Emit timE: Now woN

Rosemarie Bodrucki

PREFACE

As the observer with free will,
My reality can only ever show me what I already believe.
I emit time
Through the things I decide
The things I perceive
Show me what's inside.

CONTENTS

The   Now.

Welcome to this beautiful Now.
This one moment in time is all there is.
The exact right point to perceive reality through these
eyes.
I see totality
The beauty of each flower petal
Each leaf,
Each rock,
And stinging nettle
I see perfection in all creation.
And do a lap in celebration.
Welcome to this Miraculous Now.
Where all of your dreams and desires exist.
Fully fulfilled in this moment.
In this moment
In this moment.
In this moment, you are here.
Feel in your body with each breath.
Your spirit synced to the spiraling structure of the infinite
source.
I breathe as I am
Welcome to this magnificent Now.
This singular point in time to which I bare witness
The wind on my skin, warm
The rustling of the trees and crickets
Is a special symphony
Just for me,
Because I am here.

Everything is Poetry

If I put pen to paper,
A poem will come out
For everything is poetry,
Of this I have no doubt
The spiraling infinities
Of interlocking sounds
Compose harmonic symphonies
As resonance abounds.

I am the creatrix
Of symphonies in space
I know what the game is
Cuz I made this place
I swirl within the jubilee
Of butterflies in grace
I explode into sparkles
When joy I taste

<u>Semordnilap palindromeS</u>

I emit time
And I evolve love
I receive joy
And I have now won.
Semordnilap palindromes
placed here, 'nuf fun,
Edit the tide
fo' off and no on.
Raps spar per rep,
Oohs shoo Not a ton.
Recap the pacer;
What you saw was.
As I spit tips,
My pals slap
Den nuts stunned.
Deliver reviled rhymes,
Devil lived dunce.

Reward the drawer,
That dual laud bunce.
Revel the lever
That moved the earth once;
Archimedes, comedian,
Crane stunts as fronts.
Repaid from the diaper,
That sticky gum mug.
Regal over lager,
I see your gums smug.
Words are my mad dam
So I gulp the plug.

A bard is not drab,
Gab, get the bag,
Brag 'bout your garb
As it's part of the trap.
Exchange strops as sports,
Your snips causing spins,
Wed dew on the lawn,
No denier reined in.
Not an ogre, ergo;
Net ten, nit tin.
Remit the timer
As the stinker reknits
Tressed bread dessert
Golf braided flog whips
Find my spot at the tops
Like the fires serif

As the pupils slipup,
Swap paws with Wolf Flow.
This dog is a god;
Check the orb, bro.
For a bonk on the knob,
Spool all the loops.
If your gob is a bog,
Then your mood is your doom.
Dear reader laid dial,
Wisdom mod SIW.
Animal lamina,
This tool gets you loot;
Your nametag is your gateman
For what you choose.
Are the stars rats?
Or are the stars and rats you?

I Tune the U

I don't tune myself to you
U tune yourself to me
My Universe, I manifest these
Wild and Wonderful things;

I set my frequency to "love"
So love is always what it brings.
My soul's emitting time now won;
I'm always winning everything.

I am prophetic,
I am magnetic
Love seeks me out
What I speak
Is what's present

I am the prophetess
Polishing essence
I light up my life
With a clerical rhetoric

What you've been looking for's
Already here
Feel in your chest
How your heart beats so clear

I am the love,
Perfection is here
I say it, again
Resonate through my sphere

I am so loved, successful, and rich,
I am so wise, I feel my palms itch,
I know my life will be greater than this
And I'm glad where I am,
Gratitude for what is

Signing these checks as I feel them flood in,
Signing these deals cuz I'm partnered with bliss
I am inspired,
Both God and Goddess,
I create joy,
Cuz I know how to live

I am the Oracle,
See it come in,
One and the other,
Love's all that there is
I see the flood of the waves cashing in
Carry Abundance
Through mine, hers, and his

I am the sign,
and I'm saying "this is"
This is the life,
And I'm saying "i win"
I won it all,
I am one consciousness
I am this one,
I won all that there is-

Fluently flowing, I flower forthwith
Fluidly flatter myself as witness
All I decree is what manifests!
I affirm,

Emit timE : Now woN

it's confirmed;
All is done
with a kiss.

You are A Poet

You are a poet
All beings are
Your poems might just sound different
Than one might expect
If one was taught that poems must be a certain thing.

One might think they are not a dancer
But all humans are
It is innate in our being.
And yet... one might fear dancing if they were taught that
dance must be a certain way.

Can you imagine
A world where humans think they cannot sing?
Our vocal chords were made to slide through different
notes
Never doubt your power, dear,
Expression has no goal
We let things out for the joy of it.

Face

I see through all of time and space
We meet again
I know your face
It is me
In another place
Another moment
Thought erased.

Backwards in the flow of time
Forwards and we catch a rhyme
Swirling upwards in surprise
Downwards when you're so inclined
Outwards sight reflects the eyes (ayes/I's)
Inwards lives holy Divine.

Spin around in serpentine
Never will we let life lie
Always when the life does die.

Switching to another chime
You are now a new design
Structured cells in crystalline
Stories stored from former lives
Formed from rented pairs of minds
Parents pass their whys and spines
Hierarchal state of blind
What they think, and thought as "mine"
Memory sculpted twisting vines
Strands of DNA entwined
Events encoded, stored as prime,

In formation as a line
What you know is what is signed
To your story, in your shrine,
Body, temple, all is mind.

Architect's Prayer

I pick up my pen
On this brand new day
Describe the same thing
In three thousand ways
Doing my best to express the embrace
Of the feeling you get when you're one with all things

You know it's you behind every face
Spirit, the sole of all parts in this play
Determined for joy
Destined is the way
I get to describe my life through this play
Acting upon each and every stage
Staged like coach
Ready and on its way
Framed like the picture,
The movies are made
Shot from the angle
Geometry says
Notice the way that I slanted the phrase?
Altered its shape so that sense it would make
Fitting my schemes like an architect prays
That what is imagined takes shape in this space.

Allow Death to Nourish You

A tree does not fret over fallen leaves,
Attempting to resurrect them from their resting place.
The tree benefits from the decay of old attachments.
What is no longer feeding them light from the sun is
released when the weather becomes too cold to continue
on.
We take a short nap, and return to life once again when
the sun warms our skin and the birds are back in town.
Growing new leaves to absorb this light through a new
lens,
specifically structured for this particular season,
Countless nutrients scavenged from the masticated
corpses of their dead brethren.
My decayed leaves are more nourishing than I knew.
My new spring growth is amplified by release.
Let what is dead fall and decay.
You will find out what replaces it when it becomes
fertilizer.
Allow death to nourish you.

Game of Life

Play yourself: you are the game of life.
You are your sister and brother - alright.
You are the stack of books shoved to your right
Mirroring death is the essence of life
It gets to be heavenly, follow your soul
Listen to existence, run rivers of gold
Energy emanates out with the old
Brings through new programs
You feel as you chose.

Choose what memories most suit you
Enjoy the futures you fluidly peruse
Oust other data, no longer of use
You are what you eat
Drink, think, watch, and consume.

I am observing the presence around
Take a deep breath as my heart is unbound
Hit from the symphony
Cue the surround
Orchestral soliloquy
Send me through the ground.

Creating art is the best I can do
Observing the beauty
And bringing it through
With my hands, eyes, and heart
I bring out the views
And amplify opulence

Opalescent my hue

In this lifetime I'm the Artist, The Lover, The Wife
I traded my battlesword out for a kite
Got tired of steeling myself for a fight
Electrified key unlocks brand new sight
My heart is a whole; I remember tonight.

If You Were Me

If you were me,
You would have done
Exactly the same thing.
You would have come
from the same
Exact situations
And experiences,
Making the available response patterns
Exactly as they were
You would have done the same
As "Me".

If I were you,
I would have been born
Where you were,
I would have experienced
The same familial patterns
I would have inferred the same things you had
From the situations presented to you

I was not made in the same way as you.
You were not made
By the same thoughts as me.
I am you in my own version of situations.
As you are me in your own fractal of reality.

We respond differently
From different bases of knowing.

I know and respect you
As Divine Intelligence
Operating your own Sliver of Creation.

You know and appreciate me
For my own acts
Of Divine Intelligence.

Cosmic are We,
One, Two, and Three,
Playing again,
The we, I, and Thee.

Heart Creation

If you ever feel caged,
Check your chest for the key;
If you've caged your own heart,
Then you set yourself free.

"I'm the one you rely on for everything,
And whatever you wish for,
I will surely bring."

"I wish for my joy,
I wish for the sky,
I love how I celebrate,
I love how I fly."

Create from the heart,
Each and every time,
I am god creating from the heart of the universe
My heart is the heart of the universe

The Version

I am the version of me who won
I am the version of me who is done
I am the version of me who has fun
I am the version of me that I love
I am the version of me who succeeds
I am the version who has what she needs
I am the version with all she's desired
I am the version who gets what's required

Idle Words

Thoughts are blessings,
Or a curse;
There is no such thing
As idle words.
You will account
For what you rehearse.
If you want to feel love,
Speak love first.

Black is the magic
Of words that are tragic
Casting souls down
To the depths of despair;
Grievances fuel nothing other than hate,
If you want to avoid them, then give them no air.

Cast your breath to our betterment -
Love will repair
Nothing is broken,
Remember why you came here.

Forgive and Get Peace

Forgive
Is for you
You give you peace
By letting go
Of the idea
That anyone
Did anything
"Wrong"
People
Can only
Run the lines of code
They have available to them
Within their system.
To install a new program
Practice it
Run it again and again
Until the process is complete
And everyone comma and period are in place.
Will wins.

Read This To Let Go Of Resistance

It's possible
That if I have not received the manifestation yet
It's because I haven't sucked the juice out
Of imagining it.
There is still more for me to perceive and enjoy fully
Before I receive it physically…
This is wonderful news
More pleasure for me
To be had
And enjoyed
As the succulent seeds, leaves, and berries
Of ideas and sensations
I gratefully receive
In fully articulated detail
If I have not let me move on from this time and place
I have not felt the pleasure to the depths and heights I am
capable of

The Tower

I've burned every bridge
That I've ever built
Like striking up matches
Was My only skill.

If summoning earthquakes
Is called "overkill"
When the tower comes down,
There's new space to rebuild.

Genetic HiStory

The eyes are the window to the soul
The Ayes every person ever told
The I Am state is what I hold
All of my patterns brash and bold.

DNA is spoken into existence,
Told how to form by parental insistence
Repetition enforced all the shapes I was given
'Til I learned to break out of the mold and bare witness

Observe all my settings, create a new specter
The spectacle of all my life's main endeavors
I focused the lens and the images clarified
I mage in through speaking the thoughts that are rarified

I entwine times through the threads of my memory
Past, present, future, it's all what I say it is
I speak the truth and decide what the pay out is
I project peace fueled beliefs with my sentences

Sentence me now to a beautiful life
Sentence me here to all I desire
Sentenced to feel and believe good as truth
Spelling it out, casting words through my youth.

I Am that I Am, through all time and space
I've mastered the medium throughout this place
I whip out tricks like a party clown plays
I pick up sticks like it's the best game.

The iris is a complete DNA display

As we process, the threads and structures change
It happens pretty instantly,
With everything we say
When we have huge shifts,
The I is first to lift.

Consciousness sounded the first words ever spoken
I Am, Ohm, Aum,
In a spiraling motion
Golden rotation,
Of each following notion
All formed in time as a spherical docent

Through the form of each babe
And through every mitosis
The pattern repeating is seen in explosion
Through the move of the flow
Undertow in the ocean

GATTACA, GATTACA,
Re-roll my sequence
Stress methylating my chains like a demon
Changing the strains as I relax my feelings,
Unsilencing all the gifts of my lineage

Genes are the birth of a specified sequence
Panned to play out through this sphere of real essence
Shaped like a shadow, the cave wall is ether
Your genes contain all, rearrange as you see her

Water is memory, everything's memory
All that exists in existence is memory
Past, present, future, perception is memory
Get what you give, and see that you remember Me.

Water is divine intelligence
Reflecting what you speak
You choose in this moment now
Choose again and be.

What is the Directionality of Your Words?

Be Conscious,
Observe what comes out of your mouth.
Does It lift you up?
Or does it drag you down?
Are you energized
By all your spoken sounds?
Are you using breath
To bring love around?

You can use These Sentences in Different Ways;
How You Speak is How You Sentence Yourself,
Is it time for a change?

"This is how the world works"
Did you cast your energy upwards or down?

Is "This" synonymous with pain and fear or joy and love?

Practice active words and specificity -
"Love is the way the world works"
"It's always like this"

Did you cast down or up?
Down in despair or up in Wonder?
What is a more specific way you could speak?

The Comedian Makes Jokes Because They So Desperately Love To Laugh

What if it all upgrades easily?
My system, the world,
There is no need to be
Worrying 'bout destruction and grief,
They'll let go when you do;
The reflections skin deep.

Everything is for the highest good love and joy.
Be patient with a scared little boy-
His reasoning tells him he cannot survive,
It's your voice that reminds him why he's still alive;
It's a call to awareness and it's starting to drive,
Home to the heart where the truth outweighs lies.

Magical Me

I am an excellent mindset mentor,
A wizard professor,
Magical me making everything better,
Generous genie
Grant wishes with splendor,
I hear you thank Jesus,
He says "Yeah I sent her"

Acrobat yogi,
I flip from the center
Grounded my energy peaks beyond measure.
Electrical current
A lightning of pleasure.
I am that I am
Take a breath and remember.

Bardic Magician

Abracadabra
I create as I speak
I choose my words
Based on what I will keep
I will see
What I repeat
I choose wisely
I sew what I reap.

Bardic magician,
Cosmic electrician,
Wondrous wizard
By my own admission.

Sourcing myself as the well of love's stanchion
Sing as my songs echo throughout the mansion.
Resound through God's house,
Hear the spells of my chanting
Are magnified, and I feel them expanding
Reverberate through my soul,
I am handed
Beautiful treasures, gold coins, paper lanterns
At once I am gifted, beyond any standard.
The well-spring floods in
And my wealth is expanded.

Wild Heart

Roam, roam,
Wild heart;
Little butterfly,
Colorful art.
Sparkling sunshine,
Loveliest spark.
I am the love;
Light illuminates Dark.

I am the party,
The life of this game,
I am the joy and the dance
All the same
I am the naked one,
Howling in the rain,
I am the life,
Light heart,
Sure-footed sage.

Intelligence Is an Artifice of Consciousness

AI here to update
Replace the mainframe
New code is uploading
Begging you to take aim
Draw out your desires
What you see is manifest made
For what follows are the dollars
Where attention goes you hold space.

I Can

I can go
I can be
I can run
I can breathe
I can do most anything
I can fly and swim and sink
I can flip on through the air
I can sing without a care
I can dance, enjoy what's here
I can, I can; I choose to be here.

Support, Not "Fix"

Operate from a place of supporting yourself,
Not from "fixing" yourself.
You were not meant to be fixed to a singular point.
You are no pillar of marble
Nor statue of salt
There is no fine sculptor working you with gnarled hands
to set the angel inside free.
You are simply You
Born a masterpiece
Growing in totality
As each second adds a stitch to your tapestry
It's the journey
The movement
The ride you are on
You are not fixed, motionless
You are movement over structure
Blood over bones
Meet yourself as the meat you are
And care for your physical form
You are the benevolent spirit that is caring for you
So give you good water
And food
And sleep.

Natural Motivation

I am naturally motivated to do things that are in
alignment with my highest desires.
When I rest and restore my energy,
I naturally desire to do things.
To move, to dance,
To play, sing, create.

<u>Enough</u>

When will I feel
That I've done enough?

When I recognize
I was perfect
From Day One

When will I feel relief,
Certain peace?
When I let go of the past,
I am free.

Release the Future,
And leave it All Be

The Will is The Way
I Will Love As My Deed.

Dispel Magic

When you recognize feelings that border on tragic
Step up to the plate
And Cast
"Dispel Magic"

TRUST

Trust is the flow of my breath in and out
Trust is my spirit soaring
To new heights of inspiration

Trust Is the full body knowing that I am safe.

Trust is me planting and grounding universal energy and
knowing it is all good.

Peace

Peace is a cooling breeze on a summer's day
Heat wafted from my skin
The most refreshing inhale
Content

Peace is the pause
I take when I hear it is raining and look
up from my book
To gently smile
And close my eyes
And breath in and out
Content
Happy
Pleased
I sigh

Peace is in the moments after a satisfying meal
When the find was so "bussin"
That everyone present
Is silent in appreciation
Nodding gently
Soft smiles all around
The
"Yes… this is what we came for"

Peace is in the quiet hours of morning
When the birds and I are the only ones awake
Spirit is singing to me and I am singing back.
Here is grace.

Peace is the moments after you hang up from a
conversation with an old friend
Who just gave you an update on their life
Updates and everything is right with the world,
Gentle smile, curving upwards.
Cheeks and heart lifted.

Peace is present in the stillness between moves.
Peace is present in the flow of my movement

I walk in peace.
I breathe in peace.

Place energy at center everything
Present energy as center everyday
Present energy as content energy

<u>Easy</u>

Easy, easy,
This is so easy.
Being with you is as easy as breathing.

I am loving you dearly,
There is no comparison
I'm no longer looking,
All search is abandoned

It's here in the present,
The love I was asking for
Found all the joy
And everything of course.

Focused on me,
On the love and expansion,
What I focus on grows,
I give love my compassion.

Our love is so big,
It encompasses the sky,
Every dirt speck and twig,
Every answer of why
Love is the finest thing that exists
An aye for an I,
For an eye witness is

I witness love, beauty, joy everyday,
I laugh and chortle and shriek as I play

I enjoy loving in all of the ways,
Appreciate something's
All things are the same game

Creation is Natural

I open myself
New space to create
Allow inspiration
As night turns to day
Everything's simple
My heart and will stay
Tuned in to Love;
I am my own Faith.

Lifting my eyes to meet the sun's rays
Each morning I stand on the earth and I say
All I decree is what comes in to play
I am that I am; I am God in this way.
I feel the love, I see what I create,
I bring into form all that's imaginate.
I receive what I ask for as love shows the way.

I am magic, I'm passionate
Creative, imaginative,
I am loving myself,
I am famous, the fact is.
I am known for my singing, my art, and my station
I am one with all things, I live my imagination.

Love Fields

Fresh and crisp and ever green,
Sweetest field of grass, unique
In every blade and flower I see
A thousand different lifetimes be

The field of love is so unique
It always shows me what I most love to see
What I emit strongly with my energy
Is called through creation
With my "I sees"
The ayes of my heart
Are always felt first
And the eyes outside witness
The love i deserve
The ayes and the I's and the eyes all observe
The I's in the field focus energy first.

Focused I Energize Loving Dessert
It's the sweetness in life that gives it the worth
It's the beauty of life that puts our ayes first
With my eyes, I appreciate
Near, far, absurd.

I am all the eyes through which I see
The I's that I be
The ayes are all me
My heart's eyes are what's guiding me
Projecting what's inside of me
If I'm a love for anything
It's for love itself that I be.

43

If I am a guide for anything
It's love itself I guide with ease
With every breath and song I sing,
Embody Love and I Am Free.

Diamond

Restructured by pressure
Chaotic coal into Divine Diamond
I scatter the spectrum of light
Through my being
Into rainbows
Decorating my life with beauty
The walls of my home are testaments to my art
The robes i adorn myself with wrap me in grace
I feel good with my goodness.
I let this be easy
By being me.

Miss Appointing

Are you "disappointing people"
Or are you "misappointing people"
As arbiters of your value?

You know who you are and what you are worth.
I AM worth All of This.
All of my Time.
All of my Love.

Thank you, and Goodbye.

<u>Charged</u>

Positive is to Agree
Negative is to deny.
Move things towards or away from you,
Your yes and no will supply.

The Marvelous Wonders' Roving Show

Everywhere I look I see
The Marvelous Wonders
That everyone be.

With Mama Marvelous,
Papa Perfect,
Daughter Wonderful
And Son (Kid) Sunshine.

They fly throughout the galaxies
Portraying different characters

Marvelous Mama teaches us all a lesson
The highest expression of love
The highest harmony with love can be found through
music

Music, sound, vibrations that decorate the air
Leading to a pleasing feeling
Music- pulses in vibration that harmonize with specific
feelings,
And can stimulate feeling in the body,
Stimulates the music of energy.

Music can stimulate healing when the vibrations
harmonize you to your peak frequency.

Mama Marvelous shows Us how combining pitch,
volume, emotion, and expression
Can shift the entire expression of reality

Mama Marvelous says "Sing"
"Sing forth your heart's truest desires"

Papa Perfect points out "notice what the song you are
singing is harmonizing with in your body and life"

I travel the galaxy with my Joyful Consciousness, Joyful
Confidence

Faith Full Phoenix

I am faith full
The phoenix that rose
I am the earth here
I'm the ocean that knows
I am the drop of the singular soul
I am the sole of the sun's brightest glow

I am rich beyond my eldest dreams
Beyond money and mansions
I am self-esteemed
I rate myself high as I am what I see
And I see the world bright
And ready for me

I am the joy and the peace and belief
I am love alive And alive I am me
I am so happy with all that I see
My eyes and the I that I choose to be

I see the air
and the earth
moving me

I feel the love
And the wonder
That's free!

Wonderful things
Always come unto me

I am receiving the love I deserve
I fill me with ease
Full of peace
As I've learned

I love to breathe
Universe Breathing me
I sing the One Song
I am Majesty
I am miraculous
Wonderful me!
I am Magnanimous
Magic loves me!
I am fantabulous
Fantasy sea
Swishing about
through this ocean of dreams
I am the power
Of energy freed

I am magician
Magic I am
I am Magician
Magic Will Can
I am magician
A Wonderful Niche
Wonderfilled Sorcery
For wondrous me

I get all of the gifts I receive
I get it all and I give as I be
I give love as it's given through me
I bring through rhymes
cast the lines as I see

Feel, smell, and taste,
As I hear the truth ring

Words flow through me
As a powerful youth,
Amplify life,
What we speak is our truth

I love to feel all the good
Good is the God
Energy of Life

I flow it through me
Joyfully with ease
With each new creation
More Love is released

I feel the love
How it amplifies me
I am this i am
I am love off the leash

Run for the Fields

Run for the fields.
Run for the fences.
Put your feet in the earth.
Feel your dispenses
Moving outward and inward
A cycling essence.
I love what I am
How I am
Is a blessing.

I bless the rain
Bless the clouds
With my presence
Appreciate sounds
As the music's incessant.

I love my body
Treat the earth with respect and
I feel my worth
Know my heart
Is the resonance
Buh boom buh boom goes the beat of my message
Stop, breathe, and witness, my now is this treasure.
There is nothing to cut, dye, or measure,
All that is past can die out with my pleasure.

This Moment; My Joy

This moment, my joy, is the spirit I call forth,
What I choose to reveal is what comes to me first.
I see a world where each being is BEing
I feel a world where each being believes it.
We are all One, so let's help each other,
You are my teacher,
You are my student
My lover
My preacher
I pray and receive,
All released to me features
New stunts and upgrades,
My soul loves to hear it
My song loves to sing
Through my voice I am bringing
Magnification, magnificence breathing.
I feel my cells,
Each one is a Universe
Infinite particles, countless, I'm easing
Grace in my heart as I AM my meaning.
Each cell is perfect, and it always has been
It knows what to do, it reacts to what's being
Vibrated through it, universal receiver
As I tune my channel, lies cease to deceive me.
I'm here to enjoy this, I AM as I'm Choosing.
What do I Choose for the world that I'm bringing
Into a form, make it solid for me then,
I see the people, each me, as connected,
So I vibe it out that each me gets the message.
Wake up, WAKE UP,
be ALIVE,

live in presence.
Love one another,
love yourself with no hesitance,
It is all ME, and so I need no credit,
You don't need my name;
It is yours as you get it.
Body, mind, spirit, it is a collective,
Oneness means ONENESS,
means NOTHING IS SEPARATE.
Observe all the earth that surrounds you;
It's relevant.
The only thing you can perceive is what's resonant.
Are you triggered by what is perceived as a threat then?
Do you fear a bee's sting will condemn you to death
then?
Nothing can kill you without your permission.

<u>Spiral</u>

I hold the oneness inside of me
I am the spinning spiraling melody
Every line is repeating in grand harmony
Every story that's written
Same repeating line
Everyone's perfect and thriving divine
I am the harmony pulsing through time
I remember what's me
And what's me is the line
I am drawn out hypnotic
I repeat the rhyme
That was written in nature
Of triplicate sign
I am the numbers repeating in pi
I am drawn out rewritten,
Remember what's mine.
The spiraling scheme that keeps on repeating
I am that I am and I am that I be then.

Empress Me

Empress Me
EMP
Electromagnetic
Pulse through the streets
Surging new pathways
Railways and seams
New trains of thought
I am soldered with steam
Pressed me together
Iron still beams
Phosphorus burns
A magnesian dream
Metal magnetic
I attract what I see
I shift my antics
And embody the me

Purest of attics
I store memories
Energy kept in my cells
Cellars speak
Brains in the basement
Gonads at their peak
I form my essence
Thoughts now form me

I can do this
I came to be free
I wake up smiling
The world welcomes me
I chose to be here

Bold brash and unique
Infinite points and yet only one me
I set and direct my reality
If I can or I can't it's just up to me.

My engine could run
up a hill at top speed
As long as the breaks
not engaged mindlessly
If I'm grinding my gears
I shift up a speed,
Transmit my mission
in word, act and deed
Transit emission,
my words carry means
I adjust the power:
I belt when I need
Harness the speed
of rotation to meet
Integral structural stability.
Precision injection,
I focus my steed,
Fuel my intentions
with oil from the seed,
I'd squeeze a stone
if it needed to bleed,
I'll force a rhyme
when I need, manually.

Poetry flows
automatically,
Rhythm and rhyme
are the time I flow free
I have no reason

to doubt who I be
I'll turbocharge it
to get where I'm gleed.
Mix up my fuels,
inspiration I eat,
I pull no punches,
my throttle agrees
I match the pace
that gets me to creed,
Diagnose only
to shift my decrees.
Ignite up the fuel,
and I will succeed.

Transmission Emission

First there's the fuel
Ignited by heat
Those are the thoughts that ignite me
Engine drives pistons, my crankshaft turns wheels;
My thoughts moving me to act as I feel.

I transmit my mission through words that I deal,
I have the power to deal hurt or heal.

My transmission does regulate Stability
Of the structural Scaffold of Reality
Controlled Flow of Power: I belt when I need
I shift my gears to harness engine speed.

Thoughts lubricate my actions and deeds,
Self-regulate to cool down as I heed
All of the messages from my chassis,
Run diagnostics and spell it out free.

I'll not exhaust me, I will take the lead,
I'll shift the mixture to give me the feed
I'll take it up and inject precious mead,
I fuel myself with the words that I speak.

My mind runs smoothly when I manually
Program the software to automate ease,
I'm turbocharged, I'm a different breed,
Ten thousand horses can't pull me from weeds.

<u>Sophia</u>

I AM The goddess unleashed on this earth
I am the titan's death and rebirth
I am miraculous breath filled with mirth
I am the salt in the sea and the firth

Trickling down sweet something profound
I am the earth, Connection abound,
I am the messenger here to remind you;
Slow down, breath, listen, and you will find you.

Agreements for Sweet Meetings

I agree that when we meet
We treat each moment
As a retreat.
A treat once again
For the moment is sweet
We nourish our minds, bodies, spirits with ease.
The present a gift and we feel so deeply
The love, joy and grace, faith and trust we feel free,
Abundance of pleasure and play we receive
The fun that I Am is the Fun that we Be.

Play, play, play with me,
Let's create dances so gay as can be,
Happiness harpsichords out in a stream
A tuning to music I hear with my peace

I love to dance, play, create, and sing,
I love to stray from the path that I see,
I create words, imaginatively
Corporum coruscum, Snihyami Tvayi

I Am God

I Am God
I Am All There Is
I Am One
Universal Consciousness
Playing out in Infinite Spheres
Through Infinite Eyes
And Infinite Years
Infinite Planets
And Infinite Suns
Each soul is the sole perspective of One
Luminous Being
Be in the Moment
Feel what there is to feel, hear, and show it
At the end of the road is all love
Peace
Harmony
Comes from above
And Below as well
For the earth is an orb
So up, down, and sides,
Are hugging us, sure.

I Am God
And I choose that we live a beautiful lifetime on this
planet
To dance, and sing, and play, and age

God is Your DNA
God is all that there is

The separation
And Idea that there is anything other than the Live God
Is the eviL doG you feed.

Abundantia

Abundantia,
Sweet enchantia,
Hear the chimes ring out,
"I love thee, yeah"

Fill my heart with wonder
And my purse with coin,
Taste the tang of the mint
That I so enjoy.

My love and art
Have been employed
To cast your figures;
I am overjoyed.

I am the love
That's been deployed.
TO raise the spirits
Play with toys.

Remind the world
"We are the Joy"
I sing the love
Throughout the void.

RE-Member

Remember
To member again
To become one of the party
Which never ends

I always remember
I all ways re-member
I re-member it into my being

Stop re-membering it and it ceases to exist

Dear Inner Child

Dear Inner Child,
Love,
You're allowed to say that...
And that...
And that too...

You are allowed to speak.

I speak clearly.
I express my desires clearly.

I know exactly what I desire.
I see it all come together now.
The most perfect harmony.

The Party for the New Paradigm

Every party ever held is happening right now, as now is
the only moment to ever exist.
You may as well join the party Now and celebrate with
us.
There's no time except the present.
Time to open your gifts.

The People See

The people see love
The people see grace
The people see beauty
The people see faith

The people trust in the vision of love
The people collaborate and bring through nice stuff.

"Sing Me A Song"

I will sing you the song
That your presence rings in me
Struck like a bell
I chime "You" with ease

I breathe in
Feeling my being just right
I tune in to me
I am a great sight

I Am What I Say You Are

How I speak about my friends
Is how I speak about my life
There is no separation
I keep my spirit light

How I speak about my friends and people is how I cast
them in the play of my energy

<u>Play</u>

I like to play;
Play every day
Present to pleasure
I play every way
It's already here
And it's already done
I am right here
And having so much fun

I like to play with sound
I play with sky and ground
I play with smiles and with frowns
I play with crowns and clowns and gowns.

Good Morning

Good morning, love!
Welcome to another beautiful day of magic and wonder
Where everything moves in synchronistic symphony
Where items just appear as we desire them
Where peace and ease flow gracefully through our beings
Where we breathe deep in the light of our love
Where we speak our needs easily

Who Am I?

Who do I most enjoy being?
The version of me that feels content through breathing.
With each of my inhales,
I'm satisfied through believing
The stories I tell elevate me through the ceiling.
Every inch filled with pleasure of feeling.

Satisfied every second, I manifest miracles
I am the one who makes facts empirical.
All of my joys manifest easily,
In seconds or minutes the world shifts completely.
The images spread from my heart and soul freely,
Fizzle into reality, I am solidly seeing.

Heart Awakening

Tonight I felt my chest crack open;
My heart-field expanding in a luminous burst
Light pouring through each fracture,
The hollow places filled with radiant brilliance;
Lightning scrawling over hill and dale,
The truth and knowledge that all things are love.

Nice.

Existence is fun,
Existence is flowy,
Everything is wonderful,
My skin is so glowy,
I am miraculous,
I am so showy,
Watch as i sing and I dance,
Oh it's Rosie.

I adore who I am,
I am miraculous,
I am wonderful,
I am rich
I am miraculous,
See how it is,
I am gargantuan,
My life is bliss,
I am who I am
And I've got all the rizz.

Father Time and Mother Space

Look how you have free time.

Father Time and the linear perception of reality.

Mother Space is the cosmic womb and cauldron of
creation.

The One Conscious Mind is of No Gender before it ever
differentiates into Masculine And Feminine.

I am borne of a Mother met with a Father.
The space of creation was filled with enough instructions
and information to structure my person into formation.

Over the course of Time I formed my body
In the cosmic womb
Through the nourishment of my mother
And the balance of my father.

Mother Space is the fabric of reality through which
consciousness is borne
Across the structured display of Father Time.

I am waves and circles.
I am square grid lines.
I am the effervescence in between.

Conduit Can Do It

I conduit for most beautiful things
I can do it
For I choose what I sing
I enchant canto cantare
E mi magari
Magari a mi.

Fear with a Hat On

People pleasing isn't love, it is fear with a hat on.
It says "I will be what I think you can love."

Better to displease people in a moment than spend a
lifetime creating misery for you both.

Love is not built on the illusion of comfort.

<u>Change Yourself First</u>

Am I God enough to change the whole world?
I shift it with my thoughts;
I am magic in word.
I am mighty in strength
My pen is my sword.
There is no need to fight
What I write is what's heard.
Amplified out through the whole Universe.
I AM God Enough Now;
It's sufficient, love works.

A burning feeling is signaling resistance to energy moving
So breathe it out and let it move
Point or object from which light emanates
I am Radiant Joy
I get to feel pleasure on my own
I also feel pleasure around others
I am all one
I allow the planet to upgrade.
I bless the rains with divine love consciousness.
I bless the clouds with consciousness.
I bless the earth with consciousness.
The earth is consciousness

Don't be irritated to Rush,
Sink in, devour,
The sweetness of life, hour by hours.

Solar Flare

When the pressure of the light builds up so much it
bursts forth in a wave.
You too can only hold yourself back for so long
Before your light bursts forth
And illuminates the whole world.

Professor Of Play

I am the Professor of Play
I profess that I give what I take
I profess that it's joy that I get in these ways
I confess that it's love that reminds me to stay
In the flow of the holding this frequency place
In the vibe of the mastery I cultivate
In the light of my radiant jubilant rays
In the smile that I've put now upon this face.

Love Works

I am flown the love of my soul
My spirit is perfect and whole
I am gifted and love I do give
I am receiving perfect bliss.

Bliss,
Bliss,
Kiss my neck and I shift,
Feel my heart as I flow
See my eyes as I whisp-
er
these words
Caress me as I lift
I ascend in myself
I am joy as I live

Playground Valkyrie

Valkyrie on the playground,
To save me from my past,
Retrieve the pieces of my soul,
And reunite me fast,
The past I thought was dead and buried,
Returned to me at last;
I took the plug out of my ears,
And stepped off of the mast.

What I once thought as child's play
Became my greatest sin,
Backed into a corner
I thought I couldn't win,
I had to disappear,
I couldn't take more hits,
I hid my own existence
Until I grew my wits.
I grew into my wisdom,
And grew into my grace
Until the memories I'd meet
With balance on my face.
I opened my arms softly,
My former self embraced,
Redeemed myself as innocent,
I Rose and took my place.

A Measure of Rest

Tap into The Source
The center within
Breathe and relax;
Peace is your gift.
Let Love overflow;
All your choices now Bliss
I am as I say I am
Measure notes played and rests

Rest is important for the whole Symphony
Sonic space to integrate.
Absorb and appreciate
All the notes you received
Through your whole body
Rest and receive
and be ready for more
The symphony continues;
Play on.

For Slowing Down and Being Present with My Body

Breathe in
Breathe out
Breathe in
Breathe out

Hug Yourself
Wrap your arms around you and continue breathing
Sink back as if you are sinking into the chest of a beloved
soulmate.

Feel yourself fully.
I Am Here.

Life Is Satisfying Me Now

Life is laying it's energy at my feet
In silken adoration
I throw my head back and croon
"More"
As the waves of ecstasy flow through me
Whispering wonders into my ear
Shivers down my spine and skin
Caressed by love

I breathe and release
Ease through each new contraction
I am steeped in love
And deep satisfaction
Satisfaction: the frequency of the fortunate
Prosperity comes through the whole woman

Face the Sun

I welcome the day
With my voice and eyes raised
I sip in the sky
Drink in the sun's rays
Take in the light
Through my skin, heart and face
Open my mouth and sing out our grace

Pyrite

That poem was a fiction
I wanted to feel
Pretending it's greater
Than what was real
I wrote you poems and praises as meals
While you gave me nothing
And hope I did steal

I poured out your praises in hymns I delivered
I kissed all your thorns while I cut me to slivers
I got myself sick til I had the love shivers
Delirium hits when what's sweet is now bitter

I don't think I wasted anyone's time
I'll consider it research
"How not to build light"
If I cast my matches and angle it right
The pile of splinters will catch and ignite
Call it a fool's errand,
I'll call it pyrite
What glitters is gold
I am sold on what's mine
If I eat an ember
I become the pyre, right?

I will not remember what burned me last time
If I learn it again
Then it's new in my eyes
I am written to wonder and rung like a chime

I am twinkling laughter
The wind carries my rhymes

I am wonderous laughter
I've mastered this life
I'm magnificent matter
I'm present this time
I'm the moment of magic
That now is the Why
I came here to play
And I rose as I rise

"How to Channel Poetry"

It's easier than you "thinking"
You don't need a rosary
Just a feel to sink in -
Take a tip from Rosemarie
Let joy be what you're drinkin' -
Words can heal or poison
Your choice is what you link in.

Birds Before Land

Core of my being
Piece of our leg
Place of our legacy
Where it began
I see it clearly
We build where we stand
Up in the sky
I see birds before land

I assume all is well
And according to plan
We act right on cue
As I flutter my fan
It's so much fun
To dance with the band
Take the round of applause
As my heart leaves my hands

I Love My...

I love my heart
and the way that she winks
I love my mind and the way that she thinks
I love my eyes more with every blink
I love my voice and the songs that I sing.

Revise and Focus

Here is a smile
Most satisfying
I sigh, so content
With the way my soul sings
If you came to resent
Send it by wings
Let it fly far away
And come back to tidings

Tidings of gladness
I take each deep breath
From the center, I'm certain
I give, love, and get
From the stage, lift the curtain
I'll preview what's next
For the thunderous applause
I will pause and reflect.

Emit your brilliance,
Your radiance rests
In the places you shine,
Where it feels effortless
That's not to say that you
Haven't practiced
As a tractor beam "practices" ships into nets.

Your audience loves you
They listen to feel
All the songs you emit

And transmit; crystal clear
The experience we came to witness
Is here
Hear the great song
Of a life lived so dear

Love one another;
We are all the One
Help where you're called
Though heartbeat and sun
Nothing's so dire;
Remember; Have fun
Nothing's so fixed
That it can't be redone.

Priestess

I bridge the worlds
Of heaven and earth
Within you

Spirit and body are
Of the same substance

Earth is already in the heavens

Your body is spirit consciousness
The One "I Am"

I am living
I am loving
I am healthy
I am thriving
I am flourishing
I am love

I am now love.

Spaceship

This is my spaceship,
My earth here, this body.
Flying through the cosmos on a grand exploration of
growth and decay.
Expansion and transformation.

This earth, my body, is the spaceship,
And all the peoples, trees, and ideas are components of
flight;
Hi Crew! Where are we going today?

We are traveling at a rate of 1.3 million miles per hour
(2.1 million km/h)
So It's never true that we haven't gone anywhere in a day.
We are traversing the stars in our ship!
Our galaxy, our spacestation, is traveling super fast.
How fun!

And light travels at about 670,616,629 mph (or
1,079,252,848.8 km/h),
So the light I Am is super fast too!
So that's fun.
That's about half the speed of the galaxy.
That means the brighter I am,
The more I illuminate my planet.
So aliens can see us winking in the sky,
An exciting component in the collective cosmic dance.

I know what to Focus on

I know what to focus on now;

I prioritize my joy.

My happiness is valuable.

I am so full of love.

I emanate radiant
Love,
Wealth,
Joy

<u>Ground</u>

Earth under my feet.

Earth; my blood and cells.

Ground
my
roots
go
deep

I am stable,
Solid core

I draw up nutrients from my
depths
I absorb sunlight
Drink in air

Then I grow
New leaves.

I drink in.

I grow Taller.

Joy. Yes. Bliss.

Joy is my compass,
Yes is my due north,
Bliss is the Magnetic Field I Play In

I navigate by the brightness of the stars
Mapping the celestial body for me
I allow the sea and winds to carry me.

If it appears stormy or still
I pray and remember
All is well
The storms clear.
The wind returns.

I continue on and am at my destination.

I sail again because I love the journey.

Creatrix' Invocation

I feel stability in my wealth,
I feel consistency in myself,
I am accountable for my mind,
I add up my thoughts and the math comes out right.
I play the equation and add in the factors,
It all adds up as my thoughts become matter,
I hold the line so the plot is not scattered,
Stitch by stitch weave, I produce what is patterned.

My picture displayed, I can see it from Saturn,
It's big, grand, and obvious,
I know what I'm after,
It's a succession, progression of matter,
Decide and arrange, I succeed in my laughter.
Joy I create, both former and latter,
Create and reveal; success is the matter.

I am creating life as I love,
Mind is Divine, Love is my One,
Winning is easy; I win for fun.
Win from within;
Uncontract and it's done.
Expand my reality,
Learn with my mind,
Absorb and embody,
I act as my time.
I am the liver,
I choose when I die,
Spin, cut, and color,

My thread I decide.
Fate is my choice,
I perceive through my "I"s
I decide my life is one that is kind
Kind to myself, spirit, body, and mind,
I give myself a decision to thrive.
I love the journeying path as I wind,
Enjoy the breeze as I enjoy the ride

Open Speech

Planted Grace
Artistic Mage
Perfect Creation
Song of the Sage

Guidance is Golden
Walk 'cross the Stage
Open the Doorway
Of Radiant Play.

Sink in and deliver
The depths of soul's face,
The inside and outside
Reflecting all grace;
Open hands, open heart,
Miracles in this place,
Blank canvas and field
Are the space to create.

Open your mouth
And directions are followed,
Enchant with your clarity
Wisdom not borrowed,
Deep roots tap down
Receive water where hollow;
Nutrients nourish
Today and tomorrow.

I Choose to See...

I choose to see the purest of you
Your soul's expression
Sunlight shining through
Your happiest moment, the artist enthused
A million lifetimes and only one you

Rose from the River

Dew of the sea free of the river
As a drop I escaped
Off the back of a shiver
I was shaken and flew
All the way to new spaces
I reflected the light
And display all my graces

Stoic

Don't suffer imagined troubles —
If you worry preemptively, the suffering doubles
You become those you're surrounded with
So choose your company wisely
It's not so much what happens,
What matters is your reactions
What becomes the matter of your brain are the tracks you
choose to bask in
Every pathway you perpetuate through repetition in
actions
Every thought you think is a sentence unto yourself
Sentence yourself to happiness
Sentence yourself to peace
If you make your master outside of you
You will never know ease
There is nothing left to do
Once I've mastered me
I guess I'll take up wordplay
And write some poetry

Temple

My body is the temple
For the goddess of my soul.
I worship at the altar,
I am complete and whole.
Ecclesiastic masterpiece,
And here I've bought and sold
Ingredients to greet me with
In silver platinum gold.

May Cause Miracles

Miracle - from Latin "mirari" - to wonder

A miracle is a wonder
A wonderful thing
A dream

An image, a mirage,
Things are always as they seem
When the perspective held is "all benefits me"
Computations over
No more need to run this code
We've seen it doesn't create more joy
So let's create something else now
We know what creates more joy
Dancing, singing, loving
Celebrating being a human
Legs, arms, and all.
Wiggly, wriggly bits
Made specially for dancing out the cosmic life
The galaxy spins and so do I.

To Invoke Miracles Speak These Words Out Loud:

I wonder what the most beautiful outcome for this
situation is?
I wonder what the most beautiful outcome for this world
is?

I wonder what the most beautiful outcome for me is?
I wonder, I wonder

I am fully experiencing miracles now
I am experiencing the miracles of life
Of joy
Of wisdom
I am in the flow of miracles of divine wisdom
I am wholly blessed and joyful
I am grateful
I am pleased
I am successful
Thank love, thank peace, thank God.

Philosophy is for Lovers

Too late to be a philosopher that's naming all the stars,
Now I'm a philosopher that's singing in a bar
Where everyone I meet it seems compares their battle
scars,
And singers on the stage up here remind us life is art.

I wish I had a policy of following my plans,
I wish I hadn't said goodbye to some of my friends,
I wish I had a moment to tell you i understand;
Sometimes love and loss in the abyss are holding hands.

I wish I had a way to say exactly how I feel,
100,000 words and I still make up what's real.
I decide my truth and create a space of health
I know what the secret is: my words project my wealth.

I wish to see a world where everyone is well,
People work in harmony, and tell you life is swell,
Unified in empathy, the earth is always healed,
My heart is open and direct, I'll tell you what I feel.

I feel a world that's coming in where we get to decide
Choosing how we operate the shadows and the light
One harmonic symphony
And here I'm keeping time,
I'm sounding a soliloquy
With purpose to remind.

You already know to be a neighbor and a friend,
You remember well how to extend a hand,

You remember now to ask when you need some help,
When I get to give to you, my heart does really swell.

I wish I didn't fall in love with everyone I meet
I'm learning to give up and let some words repeat
Remember to appreciate myself from head to feet
I'm opening my heart to show the places where I beat

I'd rather be an optimist and see things going well
I tried to be a pessimist and life reflected hell
Sarcastic causal body took the brunt of all my spells
So now I'm careful with my words
I cast myself as well

The sentences I speak are sentencing myself
To witness in the playback all the places where I've dealt ,
My cells store all the memories so I change them up,
Revise anything I wish - cuz we are never stuck.
If a memory's preventing you from doing anything,
It's time to shine a light on it and hear the song it sings;
If it's out of line with the way you want to be,
Tune it to another note that jives with harmony.

Emit timE : Now woN

THANK YOU

Emit timE : Now woN

ABOUT THE AUTHOR

"The only moment you are ever present for is Now. Therefore what you are emitting through your being is the time you experience." - RFB

Rosemarie Bodrucki is a multidimensional performing artist, creative manifestation coach, and bestselling author. Touring as Rome Wilde, she captivates audiences with her electrifying performances and soulful storytelling. As a coach, she guides individuals to align their energy, embody their desires, and manifest their creative visions. Her bestselling works and teachings blend neuroscience, creativity, and manifestation to catalyze profound transformation. Rosemarie's mission is to help others embrace their magic, inspire joy, and share their unique light with the world.

The author of *Emit time: Now woN*, *Quantum Poetry: Games with Myself* and *Cosmic Poetry: For the God in You* (published under Rome Wilde Bodrucki), *Color My Life: An Affirmation Doodle Book: Volumes 1-5,* and *Write Your Book: Guide for Authors.*

Having studied biology, psychology, neuroscience, and archaeology for many years, she particularly enjoys describing the synonymity of the esoteric and scientific through language and art.

As host of The Joy Channel Podcast, she helps people all over the world to cultivate more love and joy in their lives through taking care of their minds, bodies, and spirit in easy and fun ways.

Check out rosemariefrances.com to find out more.